WHERE DID IT COME FROM?

INVENTING PAPER

by Emma Carlson Berne

Consultant: Beth Gambro
Reading Specialist, Yorkville, Illinois

BEARPORT PUBLISHING

Bearcub Books, an imprint of Bearport Publishing by FlutterBee

Teaching Tips

Before Reading

- Look at the cover of the book. Discuss the picture and the title.
- Ask readers to brainstorm a list of what they already know about paper. What can they expect to see in the book?
- Go on a picture walk, looking through the pictures to discuss vocabulary and make predictions about the text.

During Reading

- Read for purpose. Encourage readers to think about what led to the need for paper as they are reading.
- Ask readers to look for the details of the book. What were some of the steps it took to make the first paper?
- If readers encounter an unknown word, ask them to look at the sounds in the word. Then, ask them to look at the rest of the page. Are there any clues to help them understand?

After Reading

- Encourage readers to pick a buddy and reread the book together.
- Ask readers to name two things that happened as paper was being invented. Find the pages that tell about these things.
- Ask readers to write or draw something they learned about paper.

Credits
Cover and title page, © Strela Studio/Shutterstock; 3, © Uratanix/Shutterstock; 5, © New Africa/Shutterstock; 7, © Claudio Divizia/Shutterstock; 9, © Hadrian/Shutterstock; 11, © Postage pics/Alamy Stock Photo; 11, © robertharding/Alamy Stock Photo, © Print Collector/Getty Images; 15, © kool99/Getty Images; 17, © View Stock/Getty Images; 18, © Vadzim Sheleh/iStock; 21, © Hispanolistic/iStock; 22T, © Oleg Spiridonov/iStock; 22M, © urbazon/iStock; 22B, © tunart/iStock; 23TL, © Frank Middendorf/Shutterstock; 23TM, © Chaosamran_Studio/Shutterstock; 23TR, © create jobs 51/Shutterstock; 23BL, © Tirso Lecointere/Shutterstock; 23BR, © EvrenKalinbacak/Shutterstock.

See BearportPublishing.com for our statement on Generative AI Usage.

Library of Congress Cataloging-in-Publication Data is available at www.loc.gov or upon request from the publisher.

ISBN: 979-8-89577-587-5 (hardcover)
ISBN: 979-8-89577-767-1 (paperback)
ISBN: 979-8-89577-675-9 (ebook)

For more information, write to Bearport Publishing, 3500 American Blvd W, Suite 150, Bloomington, MN 55431. Printed in the United States of America.

Contents

Write On!

Do you want to paint a picture?

Is there something you need to write down?

Get some paper!

But where did paper come from?

Even long ago, people needed to write things down.

Kings wrote laws.

Shop owners wrote down what they sold.

At first, people cut words into stone or clay **tablets**.

Others wrote on animal skins.

But skins took a long time to get ready.

Tablets and stones were very heavy.

9

People in China **invented** a better way.

A man named Ts'ai Lun made the first paper.

Ts'ai Lun took old rags and **hemp**.

He mashed them together with a **mallet**.

This made a wet **pulp**.

Then, he spread the pulp out.

The pulp dried.

It hardened into sheets of paper.

□等同謹連來文如前請給過所
捉來安西婢綠珠并驢兒馬四匹
同去準狀問唐益謙得款前件婢
於此買得見有市券保白其
並是家畜如不委請責保依
市券到勘與狀同去依問保人宋守□
等得款前件馬並是唐長史家畜
是實並等乃如後不同求受重罪者
唐長史姪益謙年廿三

Paper was much easier to write on.

It was easy to make a lot of it.

And it was also lighter to carry.

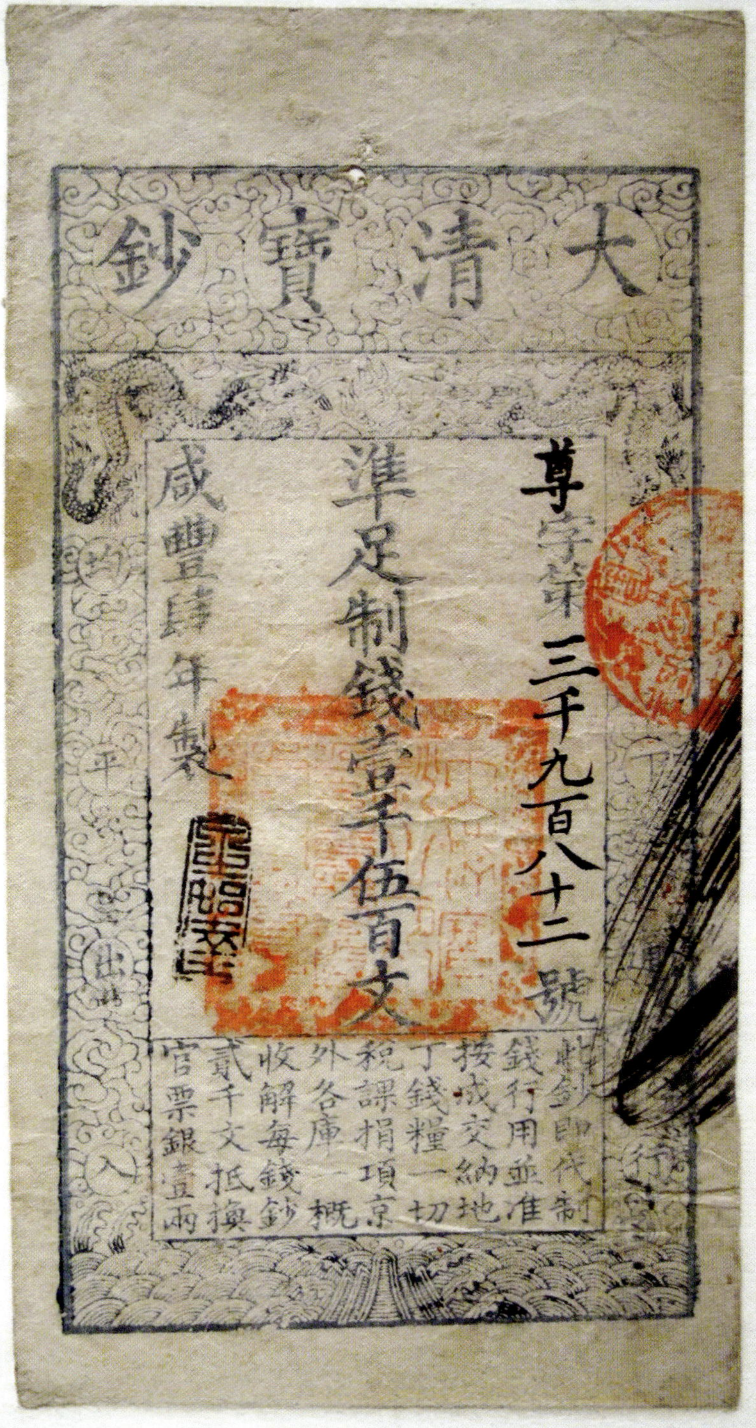
大清寶鈔
咸豐肆年製
準足制錢壹千伍百文
尊字第三千九百八十二號
此鈔即代制錢行用並准按成交納地丁錢糧一切稅課捐項京外各庫一概收解每錢鈔貳千文抵換官票銀壹兩
均平出入

17

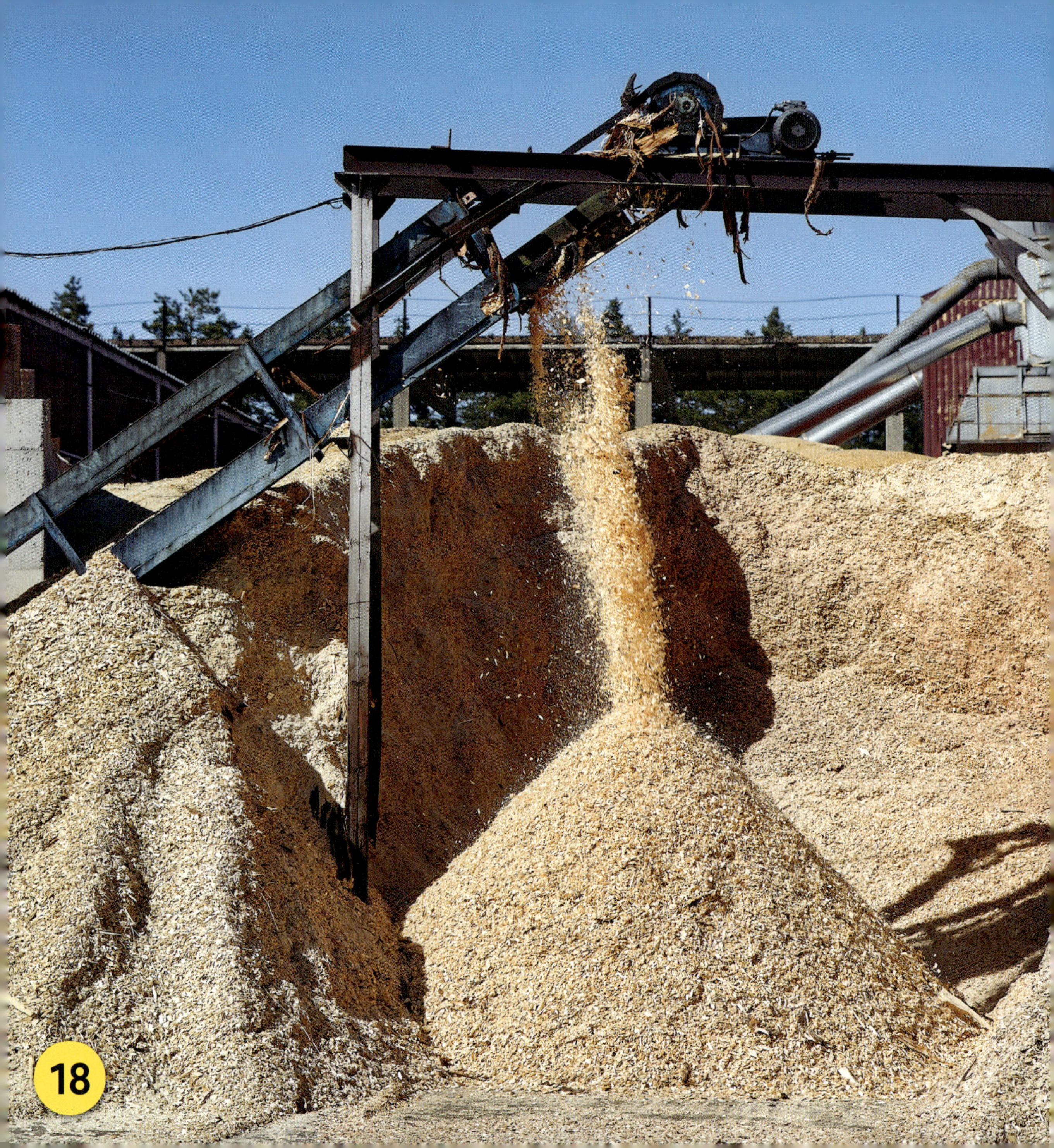

Later, people started making paper from trees.

They smashed up wood to make pulp.

Then, they pressed the pulp into sheets.

Now, paper is everywhere!

We use it in school and at home.

Take a look around.

How would the world be different without paper?

Fun Paper Facts

One tree can make paper for about 25 books.

The U.S. dollar bill is paper. It is made from linen and cotton.

Today, some paper is made out of stone.

Glossary

hemp a plant that can be used to make paper or rope

invented created for the first time

mallet a hammer with a large head

pulp a soft, wet mix

tablets flat objects with writing carved on them

Index

Read More

Boothroyd, Jennifer. *How Money Is Made (Show Me the Money).* Minneapolis; Bearcub Books, 2022.

Crimeen, Carole and Suzanne Fletcher. *Recycle and Save (Sustainability).* Minneapolis: Lerner Publications, 2023.

Learn More Online

1. Go to **FactSurfer.com** or scan the QR code below.
2. Enter "**Inventing Paper**" into the search box.
3. Click on the cover of this book to see a list of websites.

About the Author

Emma Carlson Berne is the author of many books. She lives in Cincinnati, Ohio, with her husband, three children, one grumpy cat, and one friendly cat.